Understanding Angles with Basketball

Julia Wall

First hardcover edition published in 2011 by
Capstone Press
151 Good Counsel Drive, P.O. Box 669, Mankato, Minnesota 56002.
www.capstonepub.com

 This book was manufactured with paper containing
at least 10 percent post-consumer waste.

Editorial Credits
Sara Johnson, editor; Dona Herweck Rice, editorial director; Sharon Coan, M.S.Ed., editor-in-chief; Lee Aucoin, creative director; Rachelle Cracchiolo, M.S.Ed., publisher; Gene Bentdahl, designer; Eric Manske, production specialist.

Image Credits
The author and publisher would like to gratefully credit or acknowledge the following for permission to reproduce copyright material: cover Getty Images; p.1 Alamy; p.4 Corbis; p.8 Getty Images; p.9 Corbis; p.10 Getty Images; p.11 Getty Images; p.12 Corbis; p.13 Getty Images; p.14 Getty Images; p.15 Getty Images; p.16 Getty Images; p.17 Getty Images; p.18 Getty Images; p.20 Getty Images; p.21 Getty Images; p.22 The Photo Library; p.24 Getty Images; p.26 Getty Images; p.27 Corbis

Library of Congress Cataloging-in-Publication Data
Cataloging-in-publication information is on file with the Library of Congress.
ISBN 978-1-4296-6613-8 (library binding)

Printed in the United States of America in Stevens Point, Wisconsin.
092010   005934WZS11

Table of Contents

The Importance of Angles 4

More about Angles 6

Into Position 8

Dribbling. 10

Make the Pass 12

On the Offense 14

Playing Defense 16

Shoot! 17

On the Rebound 20

Coach Olsen and the "3–2 Offense" 22

All in the Angle 26

Problem-Solving Activity 28

Glossary 30

Index. 31

Answer Key. 32

The Importance of Angles

Basketball is an exciting game to play. It is a game of action. The team that scores the most points wins!

So how does a team score points? How does a player catch a great pass? The **angle** that the ball travels will decide whether the ball hits the basket or if the pass is caught.

Points are scored by throwing the ball into a basket.

An angle is the opening or amount of turn between 2 line segments or rays that meet at a common point. This point is called the **vertex**. In sports the vertex is often the ball, the goal, or the basket.

Angles can be measured using the unit *degrees*. The symbol for degrees is a small circle (°). Angles are often measured using protractors.

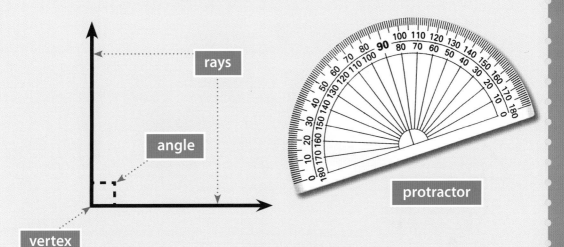

Meet Coach Olsen

Mary Olsen is a school basketball coach. She will give tips on various plays. You can find out more about Coach Olsen and the "3–2 Offense" play she uses with her team in the interview on page 22.

More about Angles

There are various kinds of angles. An acute angle is less than 90° in size. So if a basketball player is on an "acute angle to the basket," there is less than 90° between the player, the basket, and the middle of the free-throw line.

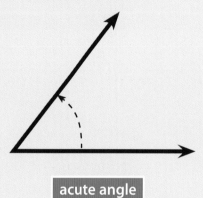

acute angle

An obtuse angle is larger than 90° but is less than 180° in size.

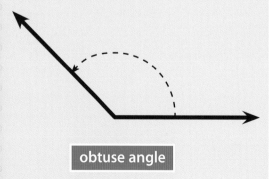

obtuse angle

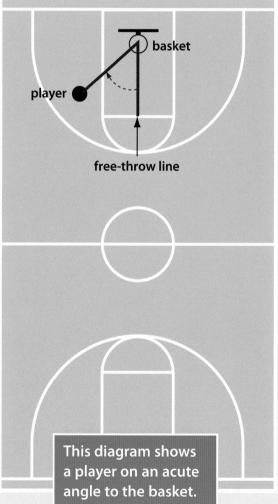

basket

player

free-throw line

This diagram shows a player on an acute angle to the basket.

A right angle measures exactly 90°. The 2 line segments or rays that meet at a right angle are said to be **perpendicular**.

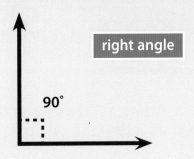

right angle

90°

A straight angle or line measures 180°.

180°

straight angle

LET'S EXPLORE MATH

When two lines meet, they make an angle. Identify the types of angles that are shown below.

a.

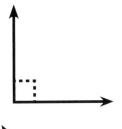

c.

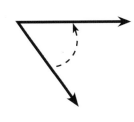

b.

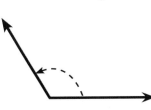

d.

e. Explain how you know what type of angle each is.

Into Position

A game of basketball starts with a jump ball at the center of the court. A basketball court has a rectangular shape. Two teams of 5 players each move the ball around the court. They do this mainly by **dribbling** and passing.

LET'S EXPLORE MATH

The diagram at right is a **bird's-eye view** of a basketball court. It is a rectangular shape.

Use the diagram to answer these questions.

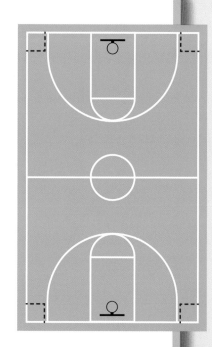

a. What is the name of the angle at each vertex of the basketball court (shown in dotted lines)?

b. What is the angle measure of 1 vertex?

c. What is the sum of all the angles of the vertices?

The Basketball Position

Basketball is a fast game. Sometimes it is hard to keep your balance when you stop and start so quickly. It is best to keep your body at a low angle to the ground. To do this, keep your knees bent slightly. You will create an acute angle between yourself and the court. Also make sure you keep your feet a shoulder's width apart. Keep your arms around chest level.

acute angle

Dribbling

Passing the ball is the quickest way to move it up the court. But you may need to dribble the ball until you can make a good pass to someone on your team.

Sometimes opposing players will guard you closely. So keep your hand on top of the ball as you dribble. This makes the angle of your dribble low and perpendicular to the ground. It will be harder for the **opposition** to steal the ball.

ball

perpendicular bounce

court

If you are not tightly guarded, you can go for speed when dribbling. Place your hand *behind* the ball at an acute angle. Your hand should be about 90° away from your body. Then push the ball hard and fast in front of you, below your hip level.

Coach Olsen Says:

Do not always look at the ball while you dribble. Try to keep your head up and your eyes on what is happening around you.

This player's hand is at a right angle to his body.

Make the Pass

Good passing will help you win basketball games. If there is no **defender** between you and a teammate, then make a 2-handed chest pass. Hold the ball in 2 hands at about chest height, close to your body. Spread your fingers and keep your thumbs and wrists at an upward angle.

Then step in the direction of your pass for extra power and speed. Release the ball with a snap of your wrist. This will help the ball travel in a straight angle to your teammate.

The player on the right has thrown the ball to his teammate. His arms, which were at chest level, are now lowered.

acute angle

If there is a defender, make a 2-handed bounce pass. Hold the ball as you would for a chest pass. Step forward as you throw. Put spin on the ball by positioning your thumbs down as you release it. The ball should hit the floor at least three-quarters of the way between you and your teammate. It will bounce at an angle. It will arrive around your teammate's thigh and waist area for an easy catch.

LET'S EXPLORE MATH

These diagrams show the angles of some bounce passes. The dotted lines show the path of the ball. Identify the angles, and then estimate their size.

a.

b.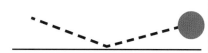

c. What strategies did you use to estimate?

Sometimes you will have a chance to make a baseball pass. The ball is usually thrown over half a court to a player well ahead of anyone else. That player can then make a shot at the basket. Keep your throwing arm bent at around 45°. Keep your other arm **parallel** to the court. Your pass will be quick, hard, and straight.

acute angle

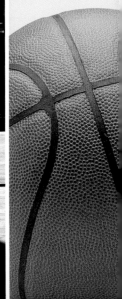

This player has already completed a 180° pivot on his right foot. He will now pivot another 180° to move around his defender.

If a defender is guarding you, try to **pivot** to keep the ball away from him or her. This means turning away from the defender. Keep in the "basketball position." Pivot on one foot. You can make a 360°, 180°, or 90° turn with your arm and elbow pointing in the direction you want to go.

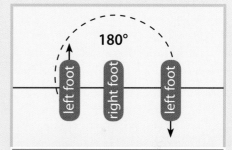

180°

left foot | right foot | left foot

This diagram shows a 180° pivot on the right foot. The left foot rotates 180° around the right foot. The right foot stays in the same spot. It acts as the vertex of the angle.

LET'S EXPLORE MATH

What type of angle is made:

a. if a player turns 110°?

b. if a player turns 90°?

Playing Defense

Good defense wins games. If the other team cannot shoot, then they cannot score! Defense is about always being on the move to guard your **opponent**. Keep turning your head at an angle to see what the player with the ball is doing.

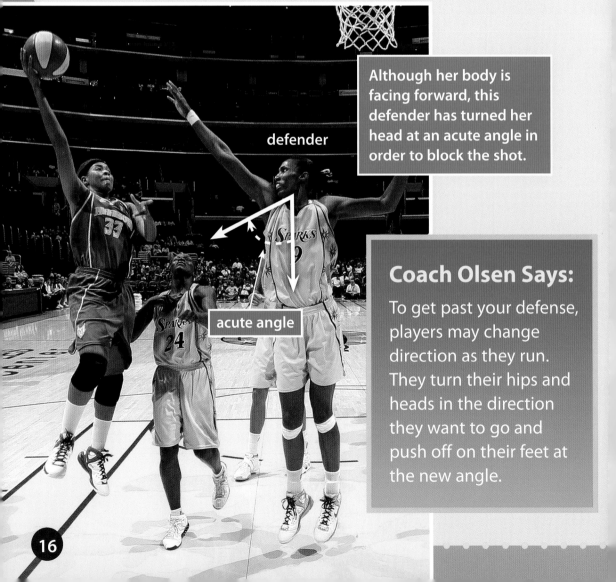

defender

acute angle

Although her body is facing forward, this defender has turned her head at an acute angle in order to block the shot.

Coach Olsen Says:

To get past your defense, players may change direction as they run. They turn their hips and heads in the direction they want to go and push off on their feet at the new angle.

Shoot!

Angle is important when shooting baskets. Whether a ball goes into the basket depends on the angle that it enters the basket.

A Big Basket

Believe it or not, $3\frac{1}{2}$ basketballs can fit on top of one another at once inside a basket!

When a basketball shooter lets go of the ball, this is called the "**release point**." It is best to have a high release point when aiming for the hoop.

A low release point means the ball will go through the basket at a low angle. A low angle is around 30° to 50°. The ball is less likely to go through the hoop at this angle. The lower the angle, the harder it is for the ball to enter the hoop.

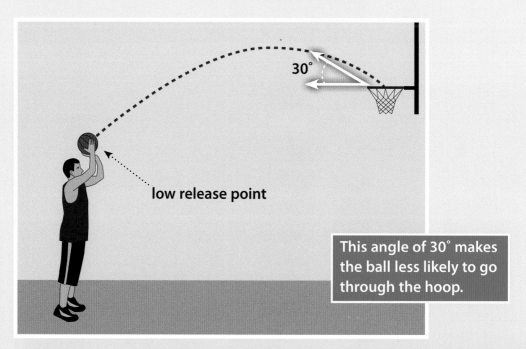

30°

low release point

This angle of 30° makes the ball less likely to go through the hoop.

The Greatest Basketball Player Ever

Michael Jordan finished his basketball career with 32,292 points, an average of more than 30 points per game. Jordan's release point was high, which is one of the reasons he was able to score so many points.

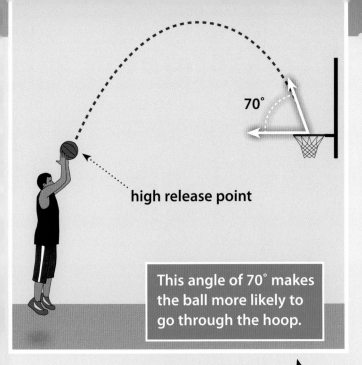

70°

high release point

This angle of 70° makes the ball more likely to go through the hoop.

You are more likely to be successful in shooting a basket if you have a high release point. This increases the angle that the ball enters the hoop. A basketball that drops toward the basket at a 70°–90° angle from above has a larger target to enter.

LET'S EXPLORE MATH

These diagrams show the angles of a basketball as it travels to the hoop. Identify the type of angle shown in each image.

a.

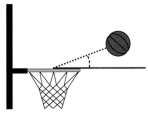

c.

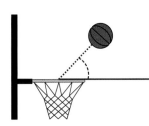

b.

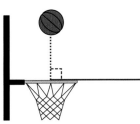

d.

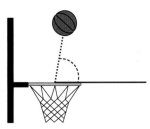

e. Which basketball path do you think is least likely to score? Why?

On the Rebound

Going for the rebound is all about **predicting**. You need to be able to predict the angle at which you think the ball will bounce off the basket's rim. You need to make sure you are the one who gets the ball first.

A player rebounds a ball after it has bounced off the backboard at an angle.

Coach Olsen Says:

Do not just stand and watch a ball as it goes toward the hoop. Always think that a shot will miss. That way, you are thinking ahead to where the ball might go next and moving into position to grab the rebound.

Seventy-five percent of all missed shots bounce at an angle *away* from the shooter. Shots taken from one side often bounce to the opposite side. But shots taken straight in front of the basket will mostly bounce straight back to the shooter.

The ball from the shot rebounds at an angle away from the shooter because she is standing to one side of the basket.

Coach Olsen and the "3–2 Offense"

In the following interview, Coach Olsen explains how she uses a play called the "3–2 **Offense**" with her team. This play keeps her players in good spots to get rebounds when they are shooting for a basket.

The "3–2 Offense" has three players around the **perimeter** of the 3-point line. There are two players on either side of the key. They keep the shooting area beneath the basket covered.

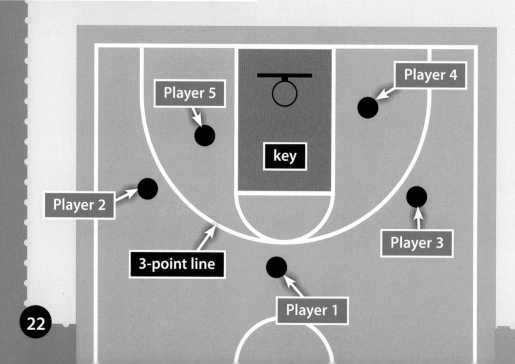

Coach, how does this play work?

Player 1 stays at the top of the 3-point line to stop a fast breakaway by the opposition. Players 3, 4, and 5 are at good angles to pick up rebounds. Player 2 can either pick up a rebound or help Player 1 stop the breakaway.

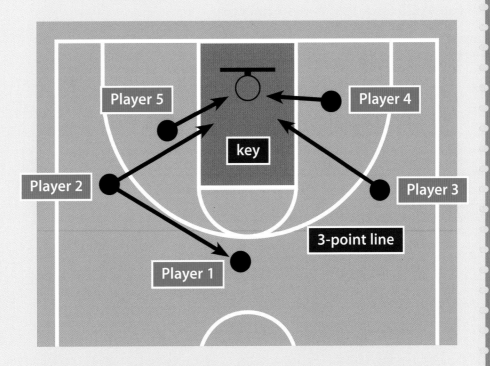

What advice do you give players for this offense?

Keep moving at various angles and keep looking for the ball. It is much harder for the opposition to stop a moving target.

What happens once a player shoots the ball?

Sometimes we score. And sometimes the ball rebounds! My players do not always throw the ball toward the hoop at a high enough angle to make a lot of baskets. But I tell my players, take every chance to shoot. It is the only way to get the feel for the best angle to use to score.

Do you practice the offense with your players?

You bet! And before every game, I draw a picture of the "3–2 Offense." I tell players to move inside rather than outside of the other players if they can. This is because the angle is smaller, so they have less court to cover.

Any final tips, Coach Olsen?

Throw the ball at an angle away from the opposition. And do not stand under the basket waiting for the rebound! If the angle is good, the only thing you will get is a ball on the head once the other team has scored.

LET'S EXPLORE MATH

The backboard can be used to get the ball into the hoop. The ball can rebound at an angle from the board.

a. Which diagram below shows the ball going into the hoop at a right angle?

b. Which diagram below shows the ball going into the hoop at an acute angle?

i.

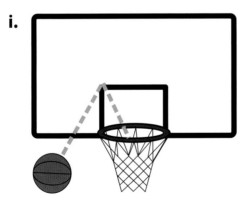

ii.

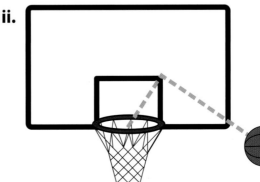

All in the Angle

On court, your body needs to be at the best angle to other players. You need to hold the ball at the best angle too. Dribbling, passing, and shooting rely on power, speed, and angle.

This player is about to make a bounce pass.

Practice passing shots and dribbling. The more you practice shooting, the more you will get the feel for the high release point needed to score.

Basketball professionals make playing the sport look easy! That is because they have spent many hours practicing. They know the best angle for *any* play.

The ball will enter the hoop from a high release point.

LET'S EXPLORE MATH

A basketball court is a rectangle. In each vertex of a rectangle or a square, there is an angle. These are called the **interior** angles. Work out the sum of these angles.

a.

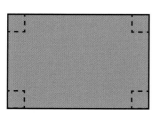

b.

c.

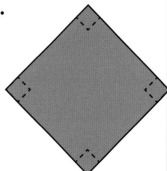

d. What can you say about the sum of the angles in all these **quadrilaterals**?

Angles in Triangles

Jada and her class have a math challenge to solve. They need to prove that the sum of the interior angles of *all* triangles will always equal 180°. But they may not use a protractor to help them.

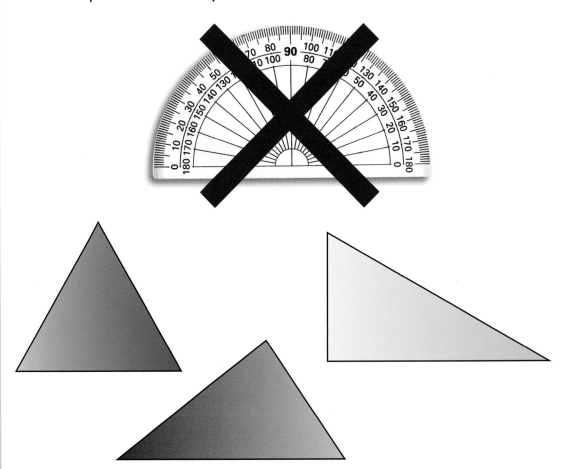

Solve It!

How can you prove that the sum of the interior angles of a triangle will always equal 180°? *Hint*: Like Jada and her class, you may not use a protractor. Use the steps below to help you work out your answer.

Step 1: Use a ruler to draw a triangle. It can be any type of triangle. Mark and label the interior angles. Cut the angles off the triangle as shown below by the dotted lines.

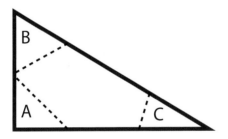

Step 2: Draw a straight line. A straight angle is 180°. Mark a straight angle on the line below.

Step 3: Arrange the cut-off angles on the line with the vertices on the straight line. Do the angles fit exactly?

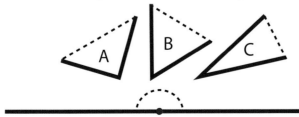

Glossary

angle—the opening or amount of turn between 2 line segments or rays

bird's-eye view—seen from above

defender—player who protects the goal

dribbling—moving the ball forward with short bounces

interior—inside

offense—be on the attack, instead of defending

opponent (uh-POH-nint)—player from the other team

opposition—the other team

parallel (PAIR-uh-lell)—being the same distance apart all the way along

perimeter—the outside edge of a shape or area; the distance around a shape or area

perpendicular (pur-puhn-DIK-yuh-ler)—2 lines crossing to form a right angle

pivot—keep one foot still while turning the body around with the other foot

predicting—working out what will happen in the future

quadrilaterals—4-sided shapes, like a square or rectangle

release point—the point at which the shooter lets go of the ball

vertex (vertices)—the point where 2 line segments or rays meet

Index

3-2 Offense, 5, 22–25

3-point line, 22, 23

acute angle, 6, 9, 13, 14, 16

backboard, 20, 25

baseball pass, 14

basketball court, 6, 8, 9, 10, 14, 24, 26

basketball position, 9, 15

baskets, 4, 5, 6, 14, 17–19, 20, 21, 22, 24, 25

bounce pass, 13, 26

chest pass, 12

Coach Olsen, 5, 11, 16, 20, 22–25

defender, 12, 13, 15

defense, 16

dribbling, 8, 10–11, 26, 27

free-throw line, 6

goal, 5

high release point, 18, 19, 27

Jordan, Michael, 18

jump ball, 8

low release point, 18

obtuse angle, 6

offense, 14–15, 23, 24

opponent, 16

opposition, 10, 23, 25

parallel, 14

passing, 4, 8, 10, 12–13, 14, 26

perimeter, 22

perpendicular, 7, 10

pivot, 15

predict, 20

professionals, 27

protractors, 5

rebounds, 20–21, 22, 23, 24, 25

right angle, 7, 10, 11, 15

shooting, 16, 17, 18, 19, 20, 21, 22, 24, 26, 27

straight angle, 7, 12

vertex, 8

ANSWER KEY

Let's Explore Math

Page 7:
a. right angle
b. obtuse angle
c. acute angle
d. straight angle
e. Answers will vary.

Page 8:
a. right angle
b. 90°
c. 90° + 90° + 90° + 90° = 360°

Page 13:
a. right angle, 90°
b. obtuse angle; Answers will vary but should be between 90° and 180°.
c. Answers will vary.

Page 15:
a. obtuse angle
b. right angle

Page 19:
a. acute angle
b. right angle
c. acute angle
d. acute angle
e. Path **a** is least likely to score; Explanations will vary, but should discuss how path **a** is least likely to score because it shows the smallest angle to the basket.

Page 25:
a. Diagram ii
b. Diagram i

Page 27:
a. 360°
b. 360°
c. 360°
d. The sum of the angles of all the quadrilaterals is 360°.

Pages 28–29:

Problem-Solving Activity

The interior angles should all fit on the straight line, which is 180°.
The sum of the angles is therefore 180°.